Sitting on the Blue-Eyed Bear

Navajo Myths
and Legends

Sitting on the Blue-Eyed Bear

Navajo Myths and Legends

by Gerald Hausman
illustrated by Sidney Hausman

Lawrence Hill & Co. • Westport, Conn./New York, N.Y.

Library of Congress catalogue card number: 75-23930
ISBN: 0-88208-061-X

First edition December, 1975
Lawrence Hill & Co., Publishers, Inc.
Manufactured in the United States of America

For Mimi, who saw it first

Acknowledgements

I would like to thank Alice Winston, whose research and writing provided the introductions which precede the poems and stories.

I am particularly grateful for two books no longer in print: *Navajo Winter Nights* by Dorothy Childs Hogner and *He-Who-Always-Wins* by Dr. Richard H. Pousma. Both books contained original prose tales which I have adapted and which now appear in Part One of this book.

My deepest appreciation goes to Lorraine Romero, the librarian at the Institute of American Indian Arts in Santa Fe, New Mexico, who kindly "locked me up" in the library so I could work undisturbed and who also allowed me to borrow a number of rare books that enabled me to study and write in the comfort of a private home.

Grateful acknowledgement is also given to Jon and Cherie Huntress, who gave generously of their time and their home in Tesuque.

Linda Nonno, Assistant Curator of the Museum of Navajo Ceremonial Art in Santa Fe, was of assistance in a number of ways, but mainly in confiding to me that I should accept my own confusion over "multiplying-disappearing-name-changing-gods" as normal.

One of the richest inspirations for the book was my brother, the illustrator, whose Navajo friends used to visit our home on Valencia Street in Old Town Las Vegas, New Mexico. They were the ones I chased wild turkeys with, and they were also the original sources for many of these poems. To my brother, Sid, to the two Rays, and to Jay, many thanks.

GERALD HAUSMAN

Table of Contents

Prefatory Note

This book actually began more than ten years ago when I was a senior at New Mexico Highlands University in Las Vegas, New Mexico. At that time I had a Navajo friend, Joogii, whose name in Navajo meant Bluejay.

Jay told me stories which had been told to him by his grandfather, who was in his hundreds when he died and who had been a scout during the time of Geronimo's raids. Some of Jay's stories would only get half-told—he would remember that according to Navajo custom they shouldn't be divulged until the spring or winter season, which would usually mean several months of waiting for me. To make up for these silences, Jay spun his own legends; one of them involved the search for a wild pinto horse that lived in the hills around his home. Summer after summer, Jay and his friends chased that horse as it moved elusively from range to range, hill to hill, always out of reach. Three months out of each year were devoted to the attempted capture of this wild creature. In a very real sense, the story of the vanishing horse, which could dance upon clouds, was a kind of heroic saga, and one which bears some resemblance to the mythical Turquoise Horse in this book.

The gift of story-telling came so easily to Jay that I often wondered when a legend turned back upon itself and was remade in his telling. Years later, while preparing to write down the poems in *Sitting on the Blue-Eyed Bear*, it came to me that Jay's personal legends were closer to true myth than were the traditional tales he told of Old Man Coyote. When he spoke of Badger, drunk among the junipers on home-brewed wine, or the young mother who, glimpsing a Navajo Wolfman looking down from the smoke hole of her hogan and feeling her life in danger, flung a wet diaper in his face, Jay was speaking from the heart of the oldest of traditions. He was shaping the words of his grandfather to fit his own time.

So these are the stories and poems which I heard,

found, borrowed, remade, or created myself. Somewhere, moving in and out of them, is the shadow of my friend, who painted a blue deer and left it on my desk before I returned east and he went back to The People.

GERALD HAUSMAN

General
Introduction

The People and Their Land

Before there was a wagon-rutted trail going north, a thousand years before, a group of small-game hunters and berry-pickers wandered down into the area that is now the southwestern United States. They carried few possessions with them and left little more behind them than campfire sites, a few rings of stones from temporary dwellings, and the language of their origin in the far north.

They stopped their wandering when they reached the Four Corners area, where Colorado, Utah, New Mexico, and Arizona meet—country of the Grand Canyon and the San Juan and Colorado Rivers; country of mesas, plains, wind-sculptured cliffs, and high mountains; country of the Pueblo Indians.

Slowly they filtered in around the settled and more sophisticated Pueblos, who for generations had been living in large communal villages on the mesa tops. The newcomers learned from the Pueblos to plant corn, squash, and beans; to irrigate when the rains were scarce; to weave cotton for clothing and blankets; and to make clay pots. They borrowed myths and customs and began to fight the Pueblos for the precious waterholes. Over the years the newcomers slowly changed and divided into two groups, the Navajos and the Apaches.

The Navajos are the largest indigenous culture in the United States. 100,000 Navajos inhabit an area that covers more than 15,000,000 acres. They are largely sheepherders, agriculturists, weavers, and silversmiths. They are a people who in spite of their contact with white society still live close to nature and their old way of life.

They call themselves "Dineh," which literally means "The People." Outsiders call them "Navajos," which may have originated from a Pueblo word meaning "large area of uncultivated lands" or "to take from the fields" or which may have come directly from the Spanish, meaning either a clasp knife or razor or a large, worthless, flat piece of land.

When Spanish influence became strong in the southwest in the 1600's, the Navajos were semisettled, living in communities on the mesas, the flat-topped mountains of the area. From the Spanish they quickly acquired sheep and horses and created a new life-style. They became herders, moving within well-defined areas with their

sheep, which brought them mutton and wool for weaving and which became their main symbol of wealth.

By the 1800's they were a strong nation, living close to the land; their society and religion were complex, despite their having no central government. The land, which they had occupied for hundreds of years, was sacred to them. Each mountain peak, river, and canyon held a place in their mythology. The grass on the plains was tall, the wild plants and animals were familiar, the sky was immeasurable. This was a land of beauty, sometimes benign, sometimes cruel, but always the place where The People belonged.

Then over a period of time, white settlers and ex-

plorers began to spread out and utilize Navajo water and Navajo land. Small farms grew into large ranches, and settlements turned into towns. The Navajos raided the trespassers, both for their goods and to warn them to stay back.

They continued to raid even after 1846, when General Kearny declared their homeland part of the United

States, built Fort Defiance in the center of Navajo country, and promised all settlers protection from "marauding Indians"; the raiding parties finally ended in the 1860's, when Kit Carson was hired by the U.S. government to destroy their homes, burn their crops, and kill their herds. In 1864, 8,000 starving Navajos surrendered and began what is known to them as the worst part of their history, The Long Walk.

With wagons for only the very young and the crippled, few blankets, and little food, they were walked 300 miles to Fort Sumner. Here they were physically and spiritually demoralized. Accustomed to free roaming, they were made captive. Proud and defiant, they were made dependent on others. Overcome by illness and starvation, they were unable to fall back on native plants for

food and cures. The drinking water was bitter and made them sick; the land was flat, desolate, and dead.

Four years later, the remaining 6,000 Indians who had not died from disease, starvation, or broken-heartedness pledged never to raid again and returned to their homeland, where they had to begin all over in a ruined country. The time of The Long Walk and exile left a permanent mark on the Navajos, and the suffering of that time is greatly responsible for their attitude towards white society.

Navajo land ranges from sage-covered desert to flat-topped mesas, piñon foot hills, and snowy peaks. The colors of the country are reds and yellows—rich earth colors, always dominated by the sky with its constant play of clouds, rainbows, storms, and stars. For people accustomed to thick green vegetation, an enclosed sky, and human contact close by, this land is frightening; to the Navajo, it is a difficult yet organized universe.

Water is scarce. The average yearly rainfall in over half the reservation is eight inches per year, usually occurring in the late summer months, often falling in a few days and accompanied by heavy hailstorms that crush any crops which may have survived through a dry and dusty spring. Water and rain, therefore, are sacred, to be treated with respect, prayed for, and never taken for granted.

Except in the mountains, there are no thickly vegetated forests. The sun shines fiercely in the open deserts; the wind, especially in the springtime, blows hard and unhindered, carrying with it dust, grit, and tumbleweed. This is not a land for soft people or for the faithless— without Dineh's belief that they were the chosen ones and that their home was a holy land, without their universe carefully linked with legend, they too might have followed the tumbleweed toward another horizon.

The People and Their Art

The wool rugs and blankets woven by Navajo women have gone through many changes in the past hundred years. Originally, they were dyed with colors made from the plants and minerals around the reservation; blacks and browns obtained from the black sheep (much valued by the Navajo for the color and quality of their wool); and occasional reds from unraveled flannel, picked up in trade or raiding. The usual pattern of these rugs was horizontal and bold.

The process of preparing the wool was tedious. Without shears, it was pulled off the sheep by hand or cut off with sharpened pieces of tin. It was then washed, dried, dyed, carded, and readied for spinning. It was often spun and respun several times before the desired fineness was obtained. The spinning was done with a simple spool, consisting of a long stick with a disk on one end; this stick was rotated rapidly against one leg, allowing the wool to twist and spin around it.

For the weaving, an upright loom was braced against a pole in the hogan or strung outside, often between two trees. The making of a good rug was hard and time-consuming work, but in the end the rug was so tightly woven that it was able to hold water.

Traders came to the reservation in the late 1800's. Many of them became friends of the Navajos and served as necessary links between the tribe and the white world beyond it. But some of the effects on Navajo weaving were disastrous. Quick to see that the durable and colorful blankets were a potential product for the East Coast market, traders encouraged Navajo women to weave

9

shoddier, less time-consuming rugs. The traders imported colored yarns and chemical dyes, supplanting the natural earth colors with the harsh, unnatural hues of a different world. They had the women use cheap cotton warp and introduced designs from all over the world, meant to appeal to Eastern housewives. Rugs can be seen from this period with swastikas, railroad locomotives, and American flags woven into them.

Today, it is the traditional rug which is again accepted as representative of the art form. Horizontal, vertical, and diagonal lines are used for design; each weaver maintains a traditional pattern, yet infuses it with her own vision. There is a saying that a rug is not good unless a weaver puts her "soul" in it. Like Changing Woman, the Holy Person whom the Navajo woman personifies, the weaver is an eternal creator who weaves both an indivi-

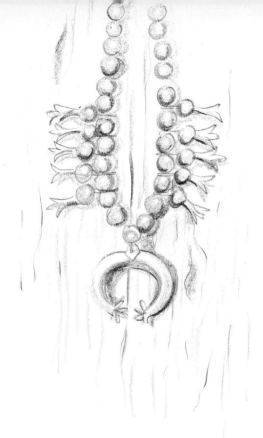

dual product of her own mind and a more universal product from the mind of the tribe.

Silversmithing did not become a craft of the Navajos until their return from Fort Sumner. They first learned to forge silver coins into buttons and conchos (large round disks usually worn on a belt about the waist) and wore them as decorations on their own clothing or traded them with the soldiers at the forts. Later they learned casting. With improvised methods they made finely wrought bow guards, belt buckles, and bracelets—a design was carved into sandstone, and the silver, melted on a homemade forge, was poured into the mold. When it hardened, the silver was removed and filed, buffed, and filed again, until the finished piece was complete. Coral or abalone was often inlaid in the jewelry, but the blue-green of turquoise was the most popular. Like a woman's weaving, silversmithing, usually done by men, was a Navajo blend of individual and traditional design.

The People and Their Universe

The Navajos have no one ruling god, just as in their society there is no ruling person or class, but rather many gods, or Holy People. These Holy People are powerful and mysterious, capricious, and capable of every human emotion. They travel on sunbeams, rainbows, and lightning. They often punish humans, or Earth Surface People, as willingly as they would help them. A minor incorrect act in a ritual can bring disaster on a man; the Holy People must be coerced to give aid.

Principal among the Holy People are First Man and First Woman, Coyote, Changing Woman, and the Sun. Changing Woman is the most highly revered and the most dependable. She never harms Earth Surface People and can always be depended upon for aid. From her symbolic image comes the strength of the Navajo woman.

For the Navajos, the natural world is divided into genders. There are male rains—heavy violent thunderstorms—and there are female rains—soft gentle showers. Earth and sheep are identified with the suffix "-mah," which means mother. Changing Woman confers female qualities upon the world, while the Sun diffuses the male qualities.

Changing Woman (often referred to with the suffix "-mah") is also called Earth Woman and White Shell Woman. She is the source of life, the giver of sustenance and destiny to all beings. As the Earth goes through seasonal changes—from the growth of spring and summer to the dying of fall and the coming of winter—so Changing Woman can attain old age, die, and be reborn. She is the symbol of the Female Rains and the presence behind the beauty of lakes, rivers, and mountains.

In the beginning, Changing Woman was found as a baby by First Man; she was reared by First Man and First Woman. She matured quickly, and at the time of her first menstruation a puberty rite was held to which all creatures came. Each creature offered groups of songs to bring Earth Surface People into being and to enable Changing Woman to create this new race and give them the power of regeneration. This is the rite that is still held for Navajo girls entering puberty. Dressed in white shell and molded into the most beautiful of maidens, Changing Woman was given to the Sun. Navajo girls, in their puberty rites, are symbolically made into Changing Woman and are therefore wellsprings of beauty and reproduction.

Concerning Changing Woman, the Sun made the following decree: "She will attend to her children and provide their food. Everywhere I go over the Earth, she will have charge of female rain. I myself will control male rain. She will be in control of vegetation everywhere for the benefit of Earth People."

The symbol of the mother as the giver of life is most important. Out of the womb of the Earth, the Holy People emerged; from the womb of Changing Woman the ancestors of the Navajos came; from the womb of the Navajo woman the Navajo race comes. All relationships are traced through the womb of the mother. The father brings about conception, but it is through the mother that he is related to the children. Brothers and sisters are related to each other through their having been borne in the same womb. There is a word in Navajo, not found in English, which means "those who came from the same womb" and which places the emphasis of parentage on the mother rather than on the father.

The Sun represents fatherhood and masculinity. His aspects are distance, power, leadership, and discipline.

Just as the earth, which Changing Woman symbolizes, is close and nurturing to all beings, the sun is symbolically a non-intimate energy source. The universe is in order when the Sun and Changing Woman, the sun and the earth, man and woman, father and mother, are united. Thus, the Navajos believe that day (union of the earth and the sun) is equal to good, safety, life, and growth. Night represents the separation of the sun and the earth and is therefore equal to danger and potential evil.

This reverence of the nurturing female has a great effect on the structure of Navajo social life, of which the basic living unit is the nuclear family. The unity of the family is important, for in a difficult and often hostile world, mother and father, brother and sister, are necessary for mutual support, both physical and emotional. It is the mother who serves as the family's center.

Traditional Navajo families live in isolated areas. Because of the small amount of water available, sparse vegetation, and the scarcity of firewood, only a limited number of people can live near each other. Such isolation makes the family that much tighter; and the hogan, which is their home, further instills a communal feeling.

The hogan is round, like the earth and the womb. It has only one entranceway, a door facing east to catch the rising sun. Made out of logs or railroad ties, chinked with mud, hogans have been the home of the Navajo for centuries. They have a domed roof with a smoke hole in the center. At night, everyone sleeps together on the floor. Although often built by the man, the hogan, like the land surrounding it, is the property of the woman.

A typical family will have a piece of land large enough to supply water, crops, firewood, and grazing for sheep and horses. There may be more than one hogan, depending on the size of the family. Everyone who lives there will *belong* to the group because of his relationship to the oldest female. In one living area, the mother and father, their unmarried sons and daughters, and their married daughters with their husbands may be together; married sons, however, will leave home to live with the families of their wives.

Work is shared by all members of the family group; work includes the obtaining of food, gathering of firewood, farming, caring for children, and herding sheep. Each person within the group, small children included, owns his own sheep, but the herd is kept in a central flock, which further reinforces the sense of communal responsibility.

The People Today

The Navajo reservation today comprises over fifteen million acres, centered around the Four Corners area of the Southwest. There are over 100,000 Navajos, 20 times as many as there were 100 years ago, and their birth rate is the highest of any group in the continent. They are a culturally adaptive, physically strong, and dynamic nation.

If you drive from Albuquerque, New Mexico, to the Navajo town of Shiprock on the northeast border of the reservation, you will pass through small Spanish-American villages, open grazing land, volcanic hills, and thick pine forests. This is thinly populated land, with few fences, billboards, or electric wires.

As you enter the reservation, you see isolated houses scattered along the roadside that look the same as other small modern houses throughout the Southwest. Some are the warm brown color of adobe, made from sun-dried brick and plastered with mud; some are made of stone; a few are made from logs. But what makes certain of these houses strikingly different from tract housing are the hogans in the yards. Although many families now live in modern homes, they will build a hogan nearby to be used for ceremonies and sings. According to Navajo tradition, religious ceremonies must not be held in square structures, where evil spirits can hide in corners. The presence of evil spirits still affects the lives of many modern Navajos, who may ·have given up all outward trappings of the old style of living.

Before reaching the town of Shiprock, you can see the San Juan River, which is the major source of water for the Four Corners area and which marks the northern border of the reservation. To the east, rising out of the

open flat land, stands the famous wind-sculptured butte, Shiprock, for which the town is named.

As the highway follows the San Juan basin, apple orchards and small farms gather along the riverbank, sheep herded by small children graze alongside the road, and a monument of a different culture can be seen to the south. A few miles across the river, four smokestacks send plumes of white smoke into a nearly clear sky. At first, it is an innocent enough sight in the vast open sky of the Southwest. The smoke seems harmless. But this power plant complex is one of several within a few hundred miles, and each one spews out tons of waste each day. The four quiet plumes of smoke south of the highway represent what may be the final confrontation between the needs and beliefs of the Navajo people and the needs and beliefs of industrial American society. This barren and drought-ridden land is valuable to both for different reasons. It is precious to the Navajo because it means home, the only promise that The People will continue as a unified group through succeeding generations. To the stockholders and consumers of the energy industries, to the gas and oil companies who preach a line of necessary consumption and increasing production, and to users of power from Las Vegas to Los Angeles, the land is a mere covering over a potentially huge energy source. Underneath the rocks and sagebrush lies one of the largest deposits of soft coal in the United States. Coal is easily and cheaply mined, and with access to power plants and great amounts of water, it is quickly converted into synthetic natural gas or electricity for the rest of the western United States.

Oil and power companies have signed contracts with the Navajo nation for mineral rights to different parts of the reservation. These companies intend to extract the coal by strip-mining. Plans are now being made to strip-mine over 56 square miles in the center of the reservation. Strip-mining is a terrible threat to the Navajos. Despite promises by the contracting companies to return the mined area to its "original state," there is little chance that this land, with its almost nonexistent topsoil already cut deeply by erosion, its thin vegetation, and its small amount of yearly rainfall, will become anything more than a dust bowl. For the traditional Navajo of today, the earth is part of the tribe, a gift from the Holy People, a devoutly respected portion of his universe. From a strictly pragmatic standpoint, the land is even more priceless, in that the Navajo nation is growing constantly, and the need for land is great, while the supply of land is always limited.

The contracting companies propose to mine the coal and then convert it to synthetic natural gas in coal gasification plants to be built on the reservation. Six plants will eventually be built, and each plant will cover at least 11 acres of land. The gas produced is to be routed to Arizona and California. According to the contracting companies, this project will benefit all concerned, and in a time of increasing energy demands America has need of all available sources. Mining and gasification on the Navajo reservation, the companies claim, will be of great benefit to the Navajo people as a whole. Millions of dollars in revenue will come to the tribe, and many jobs will be available in the mines and plants.

Some other effects and possibilities are left unmentioned: the irreversible destruction of the land by strip-mining; other and less destructive methods which might be used to mine the coal; the far higher revenue which would accrue to the Navajo nation were they to control the mining themselves; the discharge of toxic metals such as mercury into the air and onto the surrounding land by the gasification plants; the town of 70,000 inhabitants which will spring up in the center of the Navajo nation to house the personnel, mostly white, of the mines and plants (this town will require highways, electrical and telephone lines, water, and so forth); the fact that the companies expect to exhaust the supply of coal within 25 years.

When the power companies depart, the Navajos will be left with an empty town, a vastly shrunken job-market, and a huge area of land stripped of natural resources.

Most importantly, vast amounts of water are needed to run the gasification plants. Water is a precious commodity on the reservation. With an average rainfall of eight inches, the main source for the plants would have to be the San Juan River, which has a diminishing supply of water each year and which must serve a very large area. There is not enough water, given the normal cycles of drought and semidrought, to supply the Navajos, the states that have water rights, and the coal gasification plants.

Most of the water will come from the Navajo Dam, which was created by the damming of the San Juan many years ago. Over 110,000 acres of arid land were to have been supplied with water collected behind the $23,000,-000 dam, built on the northern border of the reservation in the 1950's. Since that time, the Navajo Irrigation Project has proved successful, but after more than 20 years the Project has yet to be fully implemented, and reclamation

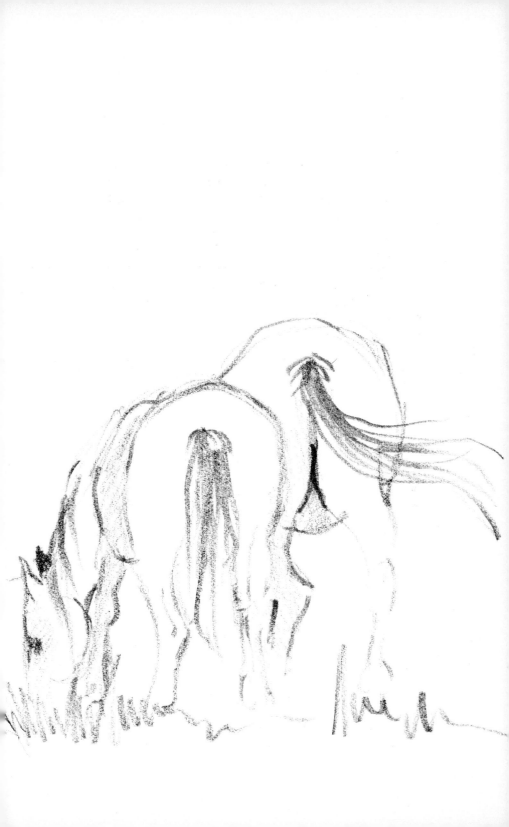

is still a dream of the future.*

The time has come for the Navajo nation to resist pressures from outside the reservation. If the San Juan River is dried up; if the earth, which is Changing Woman, is irreparably damaged; if white culture is allowed to completely interrupt the cycle of an ancient race—then hundreds of years of dreams and myths will no longer speak to the Navajos. Changing Woman, unable to renew herself, will fade into a curious design, locked away and lost inside the cold walls of a museum.

ALICE WINSTON AND GERALD HAUSMAN

*Funding for irrigation systems on Navajo land, which eventually should create a means of support for 850 families living on farms and also create employment for an additional 1,700 families, was not granted until February 1975. Water won't be received by the Navajos until sometime in 1976, and the federal government is presently debating whether the Navajos actually need the full allotment of water promised them.

ONE

INTRODUCTION TO PART ONE

In Navajo there is no single word for religion: religious life is not separate from daily life—it is all one.

Until recently, the Navajos had no written language with which to pass on their culture and no overriding social structure to bind them together. But they maintained a cultural and tribal identity that exists today, even in the face of white industrial society. The spirit of togetherness and self-awareness stems from the Origin Myth, which tells where the Navajos came from, who they are, and how they should behave. It has been handed down from generation to generation.

Mircea Eliade, a French anthropologist, said:

Myth narrates a sacred history; it relates an event that took place in primordial Time, the fabled time, the "beginnings." In other words, myth tells how, through the deeds of Supernatural Beings, a reality came into existence, be it the whole of reality, the Cosmos, or only a fragment of reality—an island, a species of plant, a particular kind of human behavior, an institution. Myth, then, is always an account of a "creation"; it relates how something was produced, began to *be* . . . . The actors in myths are Supernatural Beings. They are known primarily by what they did in the transcendent times of the "beginnings." Hence, myths disclose their creative activity and reveal the sacredness (or the "supernatural") into the World. It is this sudden breakthrough of the sacred that really establishes the World, and makes it what it is today. Furthermore, it is as a result of the intervention of Supernatural Beings that man himself is what he is today; a mortal, sexed, and cultural being.*

The Origin Myth of the Navajos tells not only where the Navajos came from, but also offers them their justification for being. In the Origin Myth, the Holy People say what must be done to have a good life; tales of the adventures of the Holy People show what will happen to a man or woman if the rules are broken; and sacred rituals are explained. The Origin Myth plays the same part in Navajo lives as did the Bible for early Christians, the Popol Vuh for the Mayans, or the Gilgamesh Epic for the

*Mircea Eliade, *Myth and Reality*, 1963

Babylonians. It both forms them as a tribe and guides them as individuals, and it is itself formed by them.

According to Jungian ideas, this myth is the joint product of the dreams of individuals, molded together through group action and experience. These unified dreams take on a reality of their own, which in turn infuses the reality of the people.

The Navajos have an oral tradition of legends and tales passed on through speech and retained in memory. Many versions of the same story can be told, and none is more authentic than any other. Dynamic as the tribe has always been, now modern and somewhat alienated from the old life, the stories in the Origin Myth continue to supply energy for renewal and growth.

Simply, the Origin Myth tells of the emergence through four different worlds until this, the Fifth World, is reached. Each world through which the beginning creatures traveled was increasingly complex, and each one had a new dimension of structure.

The First World was in darkness, inhabited by nine people, six kinds of ants, and three kinds of beetles. All people spoke the same language. There were no stones, no vegetation, and no light. It was a primary and simple world, but contained within it were the beginnings of actions and the desire for upward movement. As the ants and beetles began to explore and climb upward, more characters were added to each level and more dimension was given to the characters; there was no differentiation made between insects, animals, and humans. Usually present, after the initial emergence, were First Man, First Woman, First Girl, First Boy, Coyote, and Fire God. There was no primary creator, or God, making the world and life. Rather, creation came about from the first stirrings of movement in the bottommost world, the first active step toward change, and continued until emergence in the Fifth World. Creation, in the Navajo myth, then, was a conscious activity from within instead of an external act by a greater being, as in the Old Testament story of the Creation, in which "God created the heavens and the earth."

As the people moved upward, First Man caused day and night. He became a person of power and had in his possession sacred and powerful jewels—Whiteshell, Turquoise, Abalone, Jet, and Red-White Stone. The concept of evil came early in the myth, but rather than being viewed as a purely negative phenomenon, it was a power which had to be controlled and used when necessary. First Man said, at one point, "I am filled with evil, yet there is a time to employ it and yet another to withhold it." Thus, First Man and the other Holy People were not good or bad; they held within themselves the power of both darkness and light, just as the world itself held these possibilities. Neither perfection nor the elimination of evil were goals to be sought, the key word was *balance*.

Coyote, in reality a small scavenger of the dog family, played the same part in the Navajo myths as he did in many North American Indian tales. He was a trickster and troublemaker, an awkward buffoon, but at the same time, he had insight, and the freedom of his buffoonery enabled him to act and speak in ways that the more conventional characters could not. He played the Greek chorus, the court jester, the very pointed and painful conscience, the commentator, who forced action, who wouldn't allow the others to fall back into the dark—the simpler and therefore more comfortable world.

During their travels through the worlds, the first beings encountered many adventures. As in the myths of many cultures, there was a great flood—this particular one was brought on by an act of Coyote's. As a result of discord between men and women, great monsters were born and roamed the earth and were not killed until, in the Fifth World, Changing Woman, the symbol of life, was born. She gave birth to the Twin Slayers, who killed the monsters—their bodies are now the lava flows which are found on much of Navajo land—thus bringing an end to male-female discord. With the birth of Changing Woman, the emergence was complete. Her beneficent creative power was the strongest of any of the Holy Ones, including First Man. A Blessing Way was given for her, and the Holy People went to their home in the Nadir, leaving the Earth to the new race born from Changing Woman's body: Dineh, The People.

ALICE WINSTON

Twelve Poems
of Origin
and Journey

Before

Before the wagon-rutted trail
going north,
before the deerskin legging
with its row of silver buttons
on the side,
before the turquoise stone
set in heavy silver on a man's waist,
before boiled mutton and corncakes
and Mexican pesos pounded
into rings and bracelets,
before a child was lost among the owl people
and led home along the cactus trail
in broad daylight
with his night-shaped eyes
blinking in the sun,
before the hump-backed bear
with blue eyes was ever sat upon,
before Night Chant, Mountain Chant,
Happiness Chant, Shooting Chant,
Water Chant, Feather Chant,
Bead Chant, Evil-Spirit Chant,
Coyote Chant—
before any Chant under the sun,
before that, before that, and before that. . .
There was a hole or pit
that went down into the underworld
and the animals and gods
came out of it,
but after the fourth day of their emergence
a beautiful daughter of one
of the animal chiefs
was lost, and two searchers looked

long and hard
until they looked down into the hole
that led to the underworld,
and there they spied the beautiful daughter,
sitting beside a stream
and combing her hair:
four days after, those two searchers died.

And that is why the Dead
must not be touched, or even looked upon,
but wrapped in a blanket
and placed in an unmarked grave;
the hogan burned, and the last footprints
of family brushed away and smoothed,
so that the departed spirit
cannot find his way back
after he has gone into the hole or pit,
where the gods and animals
were born into this world.

The Flood

Now there was no sun, moon, or stars
but in the East, White Dawn,
four-fingers high, appeared every morning.
At midday, Blue Dawn lit up the South
and in late afternoon Yellow Dawn
streaked the West.

Coyote was sent to discover
the source of the dawn,
but instead, he stole two Water Monster Babies
which lived with their parents
in two large springs.

Now the four-finger high White Dawn
was only three fingers high
with a dark streak beneath.

Wolf Man was sent to learn what was wrong.
He returned at nightfall
and said, all was well
but next morning White Dawn was very narrow
and the dark below was bigger still.

So then Mountain Lion went out
and returned, saying: all is well
but on the third morning
the belt of darkness
was wider than White Dawn.

So then White Hawk went out
and Sparrow Hawk followed
and White Hawk reported,

all is well
but Sparrow Hawk said:
the water at the head of the two springs
is rising so fast
that there will surely be a terrible flood.

This was the fourth morning
and White Dawn
was wiped out
by the belt of darkness.

Now the waters rose
and all were frightened,
so the animal people gathered corn and seeds
and climbed to the top
of White Mountain in the East,
until it was swallowed up by water;
then they climbed Blue Mountain
in the South, Yellow Mountain
in the West, and Black Mountain
in the North—
and each time they climbed
one of these mountains,
they scooped up handfuls of earth
from the top
and they took one reed
from the bottom.

Now the waters rose over all
the mountains, except Black Mountain,
and here the animal people
planted a female reed in the West

and a male reed in the East,
and the waters rose higher and higher.

Then the animal people
climbed into the two reeds:
Turkey was the last
to get into his reed—
the foamy waters whitened
the tips of his tailfeathers
(they are white to this day)
and the reeds sprang up into the sky.

Now at the end of the fourth day,
the two reeds met at the top of the sky

and could go no further,
except that Locust,
with his bow of darkness
and sacred arrows,
shot a hole in the sky
which passed on into the world above—
the world of light and dark,
First Man and First Woman,
bitter water, deer spring,
and fallen leaves.

The Animals Were Sent

First Man ordered Gopher underground
because he brought
toothache into the world.

Then he sent the Winged-Ones
into the skies and mountains
to make their homes.

He told the Lizards
to make their homes
in the cliffs and rocks.

The Beavers and Otters
were sent to the rivers and waters.

Then he called Wolf and he said:
"You have stolen. That is wrong.
Therefore you are the Big Wanderer—
you shall travel far and wide
over the face of the earth."

He called Snake and told him
that he was going to be given
a bag of medicine,
but since there was no place to tie it,
he would put it in his mouth.

Then First Man called
the one who stole two Water Monster Babies
and he told him his name was Coyote.
But Coyote grew furious
over this name
and said: "Such a name!"
And he declared
that he would not have it
and that he would leave,
so First Man calmed him down
and gave him another name
which was First Angry.

After that, Coyote felt better;
he had been given a great name,
or so he thought,
and he went away happy,
because he was told
that whatever happened
on the face of the earth,
he would be the first to know.

Eagle-Death

Elder Brother came to the mountain
of the Eagles. "When will your father
come?" he asked the two nestlings.
"When the man's rain falls,"
they answered. And when the Father
Eagle came, he threw a young man
on a rock and that was where
Elder Brother killed the Father Eagle
with an arrow.

"When will your mother come?" he
asked the two nestlings. "When
the woman's rain falls," they answered.
And when the Mother Eagle came,
she threw down a beautiful girl with
long hair and strings of turquoise
for earrings. When Elder Brother shot
the Mother Eagle through the heart,
her terrible cry was heard on four
mountains. After the last echo died,
he turned and faced the frightened
nestlings and said:

> "Sit here before me.
> From this day
> you will not think
> as your father thought;
> your mother's thoughts
> have flown from you.
> Forget that other life
> and those white flowers
> of your feather quilt.
> Your mother and father
> will enter you no more.
> The tribe called The People
> will use you—
> they will wear your claws,
> dance with your feathers
> and see with your fast eyes.
> You belong to us now."

The Evil Eye

There was a rock with a Black Hole
and Elder Brother went there
and looked within.
What he saw were a whole family
of Evil Eyes
looking up at him.
He built a fire beside Black Hole
and with a bag of salt,
he made a great billow of smoke
which hurt the Evil Eyes
and made harsh tears
run down their upturned faces;
then they could not see
and Elder Brother killed them.
From these beings came the trouble
of sore eyes amongst The People,
and Elder Brother prayed
there would be no more beings
with the Evil Eye.

The Younger Sister
and the Blue Racer Snake

The Younger Sister was very tired,
her mocassins worn thin,
her clothing in rags.

She could see smoke from the Great Snake's
smoke-pipe close behind her.

She ran until she came to a place
called Sage Canyon.
There she almost stepped upon
a slender young man with a bluish face,
sunning himself on a rock.

"I am called Blue Racer," he said,
"Where are you going in such a hurry?"

"I am being chased by the Great Snake,"
she said.

"No Great Snake comes here,"
he laughed confidently.
"Take off your ragged clothes
and come with me."

She went to the young man naked
and he blew into a tiny hole
four times
until it was large enough
for both to enter.

When Great Snake came to the place
where the Younger Sister

had shed her clothes,
he grabbed them up in his mouth
and hissed:
"Oh, my wife! My wife!"

But Blue Racer spoke through the tiny hole,
which was too small
for Great Snake to enter,
and told him to go away.

The power of his words
was too much for Great Snake
and he was forced to turn around
and go home.

That night, Blue Racer dressed

in his finest snake's skin
and came forward
to meet Younger Sister,
who wished at that moment
to go outside.

She tried to leave, but a throng of snakes
blocked her path;
they were on all sides of her,
so she threw herself
on the ground.

Next morning, the snake people
complained bitterly.
One said: "Sister-in-law is not kind,
she stepped on my neck."
Another said: "She stepped on my arm."
And another: "She hurt my leg."

Later, she had a pain in her stomach;
they gave her medicine
and she was quiet.

Then came her children:
a boy-child-snake
and a girl-child-snake.

And that is why a Navajo
who sees a snake
crawling on the ground
or sunning itself on a rock,
calls it by name,
and sends it very gently away.

Shiprock

The Utes were after him
and the young man was fearful.

He came to a river
and the water lifted
and the young man
went under it
to the home of the otter.

The otter said:
"The enemy will not come here.
You are safe."

The Utes searched the country
but they could not find the young man.

So he left the home of the otter
and moved into a new country
and again he grew fearful
that the Utes had found his track.
As he ran, he cried
and someone called to him
from a tree.

A round voice said:
"Why do you cry?"

The young man answered:
"The Utes are after me.
They want my scalp."

The voice said:

"Come up here, Grandchild.
They will not follow
you here."

The young man climbed the tree
and he entered the home of the owl.
The owl circled the tree
four times and he sprinkled
sun-medicine
to hide the young man.

The Utes hunted around
and around the tree
but they found nothing
and finally they went away.

The young man again set out
to find his home country,

but he traveled very far
out of his way
and moved in circles so he was lost
with tears in his eyes
when he heard someone
speak to him.

This time the white ground squirrel
called to him
and lifted up a greasewood bush
and blew four times under it.

Then he went down into the hole
and the young man followed
and was soon safe from his enemies,
the Utes, but after he came out of the hole
he got lost again
in another strange country.
As his eyes filled with tears,
he heard a small voice
coming from under the rocks:

"Why do you cry?" it asked.

"Because the Utes are after my scalp."

This time a mountain rat
spoke to the young man.

"Nevermind," it said. "They never
enter my house."

And he quickly opened his home
under the rocks
and the young man passed through,
and the rocks were sealed in place.

Again the Utes searched all over,
and again they did not find him.

After the Utes went away,
the young man came out into the sun
and walked very far.
He reached the San Juan River
and the water was high.
He walked along the riverbank,
eating berries that grew there.
He heard someone behind him.

A voice said:
"Grandson, what are you doing here?"
The young man turned
and looked into the face
of a Man of Dark Color.

"I have come far," he answered,
"from the country of the Utes.
I am trying to reach my home,
but the river is high
and I cannot cross."

"Shall I take you across?"
said the Dark Man.

The young man climbed on his back.

When the two had crossed
the San Juan River safely
and the young man had been put down
gently,
the Dark Man turned into a black rock
that grew and grew,
while his arms spread out
into great wings.

He is there to this day:
The Rock with Wings,
Shiprock.

The Whistle

At first the man rubbed
yucca fruit and sacred waters
over the woman's heart.
Then she did the same to him,
and this was good
except Jealousy came
from somewhere
and man and woman
were kept apart.

A medicine was prepared,
which made man and woman
whistle between the legs.

After that, they were together again
and the whistle's pitch was different.

That is why a boy's voice
and a girl's voice are not the same:
that is why voices change
and other things happen,
over and over.

Growing Old

First Man and First Woman
did what was best
for the Sky, the Earth, and The People.
But after Coyote's bad conduct
their work went sour.

This is how it goes:

The People's hair was supposed
to remain black like the crow,
but one day, there came
a bird-person with white head,
whose name was Nuthatch.

He spoke:"Grandchildren,
look here, I am turning grey;
I am growing old."

When he flew away
the dust of his wings
fell upon The People's hair
and they knew there was such a thing
as old age.

But The People's teeth
were still white, and strong, and clean—
First Man and First Woman
had made it so:
white teeth for white corn.

One day, Old Man Gopher
came with face

all puffed out in pain.

"Oh, Grandchildren," he groaned,
"I have a toothache,
pull my bad teeth for me."

So The People pulled his bad teeth
until only the two front ones
were left.
And from that time on,
The People knew what it was like
to have a toothache.

That is why The People
now wear the topfeathers
of the Nuthatch
and have grey hairs;
and that is why
they rub their cheeks
when Old Man Gopher
pops out of his hole.

The Visit of the Holy Person

"I was sitting here today
when suddenly everything turned
bright white inside the hogan.
I turned and saw a handsome man.
He asked about you, my son.
I told him you stay away
all day because the girls tease you.
He asked what we ate
and where we slept.
I showed him the seed cakes I made
and the rabbits you killed.
I showed him our woven mat beds.
Then he reached out
for a piece of bread and he spoke:
'This is my food also.'
As soon as he said this,
he was gone
and there was nothing
left of him
except the piece of seed cake
and a single track
outside the door."

Rainbow

When I cross the deep canyon
with nowhere in its belly
and nothing in its heart
I throw over my friend
Rainbow
and walk soft
as a young deer
upon a rainy-colored spine.

The Turquoise Horse

I am the Sun's son.
I sit upon a turquoise horse
at the opening of the sky.

My horse walks on terrifying hooves
and stands on the upper circle of the rainbow
with a sunbeam in his mouth
for a bridle.

My horse circles all the peoples of the earth.

Today, I ride on his broad back
and he is mine;
Tomorrow he will belong to another.

ABOUT THE POEMS

Before

"Before the hump-backed bear with blue eyes was ever sat upon" refers to the bear from a sand painting used in the Mountain Top Way. Sand paintings are intricate dry paintings done on the floor of the hogan before a ceremony. The patient sits upon the painting as part of the cure: he draws strength from it and is reborn.

Gods or Holy People and animals emerged from the underworld at the same time. The animals and insects have both magical powers and human characteristics: thus Coyote is a trouble-causer; Wolf, a thief. Most animals are considered positive forces and are referred to as brother and sister.

The last stanza describes some of the ritual which must be undergone when a person has died and the body must be disposed of.

The number four repeats itself in Navajo ritual. There are four directions, the four seasons, the four colors, and substances associated with the four sacred mountains. White and white shell indicate the east; blue and turquoise, the south; yellow and coral, the west; black and jet, the north. Other significant numbers are five and nine.

Coyote is present here as the eternal trickster and trouble-causer. But his mischief has a dual effect. It brings the dangerous and negative reaction of the flood, but also, because of the flood, forces the people up into a more complex and promising world.

Corn is the most important crop to the Navajo and to other western Indians. It originated in the New World and is the only primary grain (the others being rice and wheat) which must be cultivated. It is considered sacred and lifegiving. Corn pollen is sprinkled on the patient during chants; corn meal is eaten in the marriage ceremony. There is both male and female corn.

The mountains are the four sacred mountains which border the Navajo lands: Mount Blance (Sisnaajini) to the east; Mount Taylor (Tsoodzil) to the south; the San Francisco peaks (Doko'oosliid) to the west; and Mount Hesperus (Dibentsaa) to the north.

Eagle-Death

The Man's Rain, represented by the Sun, is the violent thunderstorm which drives the seed into the ground. The Woman's Rain is the gentle rain that nurtures the soil and brings forth the crops. It is represented by Changing Woman.

The Evil Eye

Elder Brother, who is the son of Changing Woman and the bolder member of the Twin Slayers (also known as Hero Twins), kills the monsters who trouble The People.

In "Eagle Death" and "The Evil Eye" what is actually happening is a mythological purging of abnormal sex forces. According to Frank Waters in his book, *Masked Gods*, it was during the mythical time of the separation of the sexes that the women practiced masturbation, and from this act produced monsters as offspring. These monsters were the result of a misapplication of the sexual life force, which is synonymous with the power of the sun. It was the Sun Father who instructed Elder Brother and his weaker twin to destroy the monsters and to prepare for the coming of the new race of Navajos.

On a more universal level, both poems speak of man's effort to harmonize body, mind and heart with divine will.

Shiprock

The Utes are Plains Indians with whom the Navajos often

came in contact, traded, intermarried, and fought. Their country formed the northern border of Navajo land. Once on the other side of the San Juan River, the Navajo was in enemy territory. Shiprock, standing high on the plains, is like a sign that the Navajo is safe within his own country.

Growing Old

First Man and First Woman are two of the more important of the Holy People. First Man assigned the different animals to their positions in the world; he caused light and dark to come about; together with First Woman, he reared Changing Woman.

The Visit of the Holy Person

Navajos who have seen Holy People will offer proof of this in the appearance of a single footprint in the sand.

Rainbow

The rainbow is the path of the Holy People, or Yei, and is depicted in sand paintings. During the stormy summer months, rainbows are an almost constant phenomenon, stretching very clear and bright across the vast sky, sometimes two or three rainbows appearing at the same time.

The Turquoise Horse

Since the horse was not indigenous to the western hemisphere, its arrival brought a wholly new way of life to most of the Indian tribes. It came to signify power and speed and wealth.

A.W.

Two Stories
of the
Winter Fire

Rain Boy and Butterfly Boy

There is a great arch of colored stone in Navajo Country, and it is called Rainbow Bridge. In order to reach it you must ride horseback for days through desert and bare rock land and through great red rock canyons. Not many people go there. In ancient times it was the home of Rain Boy, a powerful god, whose weapon was lightning and who traveled as fast as the wind on his rainbow.

One day long ago he had to go on a journey. He left his wife and daughter at home at Rainbow Bridge and told them that no matter what happened they were not to go out into the sunlight.

"We will obey you, Rain Boy," said the two women, and when he had gone they sat by the open door and took up their weaving. They were both fine weavers. When they needed a new design they would look out of the door until they saw something beautiful. One day, it was the design of a leaf; another day, a bird feather suited their needs. But today they could not see anything that pleased them.

As it happened, White Butterfly Boy had flown into their part of the country from his home in Chaco Canyon, where the ruins of the dead people lie. Butterfly Boy looked just like a Navajo except that he had wings. He possessed one other great power. He could change himself at will into a white butterfly. Today when he came to Rainbow Bridge he saw the beautiful wife and daughter of Rain Boy looking out of the door of their hogan.

"They are beautiful. I should like to talk to them," he said to himself, but he had heard that Rain Boy wouldn't let them talk to strangers and forbade them to leave the hogan when he was away. So Butterfly Boy planned a trick; he changed himself into a white butterfly and flew down onto the door sill.

"Oh, what a beautiful creature," cried the mother. "What a splendid design he will make for our weaving."

"Let us catch him," said the daughter.

But when they reached out with their hands, White Butterfly Boy spread his wings and flew to a milkweed blossom some distance from the hogan. The women forgot their promise to Rain Boy and ran out of the house into the sunlight where they chased the sparkling white butterfly; each time they got near enough to catch him, away he flew, farther from the hogan. Four times he flew, and the fourth time he lit on a tassel of corn silk in Rain Boy's garden. Great yellow pumpkins coiled their arms between the corn stalks, and when the women ran into the garden the pumpkins caught them, so they could not take another step. Then Butterfly Boy turned himself into a man with wings.

"There," he said. "I have you. Now you will come live with me in Chaco Canyon."

He took them far off over the desert and canyon until they came to the land of deserted hogans. Here, long ago, people had lived, but now nothing but the dead remained, and they were buried deep under the blown sands.

Now, Rain Boy returned from his journey, and finding the hogan empty, he searched outside for tracks. In the sands by the hogan he saw footprints of his wife and daughter, which led into the garden and among the pumpkin vines where they disappeared. It was here that White Butterfly Boy had turned into a man with wings, and with Rain Boy's wife on one arm and the daughter on the other, he had flown back to his home in Chaco Canyon. After looking carefully among the corn stalks, Rain Boy sent out a streak of lightning to point the direction they had taken. The lightning struck near Chaco Canyon. Rain Boy mounted his rainbow and rode over the sky to the home of White Butterfly Boy. There he found his wife and daughter, who were prisoners in the hogans of the ancient people. Rain Boy was very angry with them for disobeying him, but he was even more angry with White Butterfly Boy for his treachery.

When White Butterfly Boy came flying home at night, Rain Boy said, "I challange you to a race. If you win, you may keep my wife and daughter. If you lose, you die."

"I agree," said White Butterfly Boy.

"We shall race to Mount Taylor," said Rain Boy. "Get ready. When I send out my lightning we shall start."

Now Butterfly Boy had nothing in the world to race upon but his own wings, so he spread them out proudly and waited with his only weapon which was a magic axe

that could kill whoever held it, at a puff of breath.

Rain Boy took off on his bolt of lightning and was gone instantly. Butterfly Boy beat his wings as fast as he could, but it was going to take him a long time to reach Mount Taylor. On the way, he saw Humming Bird poised in the air before a flower.

There is nothing in the world that Butterfly Boy liked more than to have fun. About his throat hung a tiny silver bell. He wanted to hear how the bell would sound on the throat of Humming Bird as he darted from blossom to blossom, so he took the bell from his own throat and threw it into the air. It dropped with a tinkle onto Humming Bird's neck; this is the noise you hear today when Humming Bird rushes in upon a flower.

Soon after his delay with Humming Bird, Butterfly Boy reached Mount Taylor. There sat Rain Boy on the end of a streak of lightning.

"I win," cried Rain Boy. "Now we will race back again."

"All right," said Butterfly Boy tiredly. By now he was already exhausted, but he was cheerful and did not give up. Again he spread his beautiful wings.

"Ready?" shouted Rain Boy, and this time he rode up over the sky on a great rainbow. Butterfly Boy strained himself to fly, but it was a long time before he reached his home in Chaco Canyon. There sat Rain Boy on the end of the rainbow, and his wife and daughter were waiting beside him.

"I win again," Rain Boy said, and raising his head he proclaimed: "now you will die!"

"Wait," said Butterfly Boy. "Won't you please kill me with my own axe? It would make me happy to die by the blade I have carried on my journeys."

But Rain Boy knew that Butterfly Boy's axe was a magic axe. At a puff of breath from its master it would fly back and kill the man who held it.

"No," he said, "I will kill you with my own axe." And again he raised it above his head. But Butterfly Boy begged four times, and the fourth time Rain Boy stuck his own axe in his belt and took the magic axe in his hand. But he was not to be tricked. He had a scheme in mind.

"Now," said clever Rain Boy, "close your eyes."

As soon as Butterfly Boy had shut his lids Rain Boy changed axes, and grasping his own trusty weapon he hit Butterfly Boy a deadly blow on the head. The skull cracked, Butterfly Boy was killed at one stroke, and out of the crack in the skull came a net of butterflies, all bright-winged and lovely. Away they flew to scatter over the sky; and that is how the beautiful butterflies of this world came to be born.

Coyote and Beautiful Woman

Long ago there lived a Beautiful Woman, who was the sister of 12 divine brothers. She had many handsome suitors but none could win her.

One day Ma-i, the Coyote, thought he would see if the stories of her beauty were true, so he trotted across hills and valleys to her hogan. When he saw her his eyes grew terribly large and he said without thinking, "What must I do to win your hand?"

"It would be of no use for you to know; you couldn't satisfy my demands."

Coyote believed there was nothing in the world which he couldn't do.

"Tell me," he said, "what must I do?"

"All the others have failed; how could you succeed?"

Coyote would not give up. A third time he asked, "Please tell me what I must do to win your hand?"

She repeated, "You cannot win my hand. You are not big enough or strong enough."

"Please tell me," said Coyote in desperation, "I will do anything you ask."

Now on the fourth time he asked, Beautiful Woman answered, "The person who marries me must first kill a giant."

Coyote went away immediately and devised a plan; the next day he started out to find a giant. After a short time he met Grey Giant, who was half as big as Big Pine, with an evil eye and long yellow tusks for teeth.

"Grey Giant," Coyote shouted, because the giant's ears were so far above him, "do you know why you cannot catch all of your enemies? You cannot run fast enough. I can jump over four bushes in one bound." Coyote jumped over four sage bushes to show off.

"Cousin Coyote," said Grey Giant in a low resonant voice, "how is it that you can run so well?"

"I will tell you the secret," answered Coyote quickly. "But first you must build a sweat house so that we may purify ourselves."

"All right, Cousin, I'll build a sweat house," said Grey Giant, and he set to work carrying logs and putting them up tent fashion and plastering the chinks with mud.

Coyote went off and hunted until he found the thigh bone of an antelope that Mai-t'so, the wolf, had killed and eaten. He hid it under his fur coat. When he returned, the sweat house was finished. Together, he and Grey Giant built a fire and heated rocks and made a leaf carpet for the floor. Coyote hung the four blankets of the sky over the doorway—one white, one blue, one yellow, and one black. It made the sweat house dark as night inside. They took off their clothes and hung them with their weapons on Big Pine; then they entered the sweat house and sat down.

"Now," said Coyote, "do as I say and you will become a fast runner. Cut the flesh off your thigh to the bone, and then break the bone, I will cut mine first to show you how."

"Doesn't it cause much pain?" asked Grey Giant, stupidly.

"That part is soon over," replied Coyote. "And afterward you will become a fast runner." Then Coyote reached for a great stone knife and pretended to cut his thigh.

He howled and he yowled, so that the sweat house shook with the vibrations. "Ahg! What pain!" he cried, as he prayed and sang, and he pretended to slash his leg some more. "Now I have to cut my leg to the bone," said Coyote.

It was dark as night in the sweat house and Grey Giant couldn't see a thing; Coyote put the old bone on top of his thigh and thrust it toward Grey Giant.

"There, you can feel my bone laid bare. Feel it with your hand."

Grey Giant put his hand on Coyote's leg and felt the

antelope bone that Coyote had smuggled into the house.

"It is true. You have cut away the flesh to the bone," said Grey Giant, stupified.

"I do it often to make myself a fleet runner," said Coyote. "Now comes the worst part. I must break my bone."

He held the stone knife above his head and brought it down with all his strength. Crack! The bone splintered into pieces. Coyote howled and prayed.

"Feel it, Grey Giant, feel it!"

Grey Giant felt the broken ends which had scattered on the floor. "What you say is true enough, Cousin, but doesn't it hurt awfully bad?"

"Yes," snapped Coyote. "But this is why I'm the fastest runner in the world." Coyote spit on his thigh and sang: "Tohe! Tohe! Tohe! Heal together! Grow together! Tohe! Tohe! Tohe!" In a short time he said, "Grey Giant," feel my leg. It is well. I can run faster than ever now."

Grey Giant felt the leg all over.

"I will do as you have done. I too want to become a fast runner."

"Here is the knife," said Coyote, and Grey Giant took the stone knife and began to cut away the skin on his thigh. He howled in a voice like thunder.

"Never mind if it hurts," said Coyote. "Remember that you will soon be a fast runner. Keep right on cutting."

Grey Giant roared and howled but he kept on cutting until, scratch, he reached the bone.

"Cousin, I am now at the bone," said Grey Giant.

"Now," said Coyote, "break the bone."

Giant gave his leg a mighty whack with the stone knife. The bone cracked and shattered into pieces.

"It is done," roared Grey Giant, and he commenced to pray and sing as Coyote had done. He held the two parts of the leg together.

"Tohe! Tohe! Tohe! Heal together! Grow together! Tohe! Tohe! Tohe! Help me, Coyote. Help me, Cousin. The bone doesn't heal."

Coyote saw that it was time for him to leave. He ran out of the sweat house and fetched his bow and arrows. He took away the sky blankets from the door and shot several arrows into Grey Giant, who fell to the floor with a wounded heart and died soon after.

Coyote cut off his scalp with the stone knife and hung it on the end of a cedar stick. Giants are the only people in Navajo country with yellow hair and Coyote knew that Beautiful Woman would recognize the giant's scalp; but to make sure he took the giant's great quiver and arrows for further proof of his cunning act.

When he reached the hogan of Beautiful Woman, he threw the trophies at her feet, the yellow-haired scalp, the great quiver, and the arrows.

"Now, Beautiful Woman, I have killed a giant. I have come for my reward. Marry me," said Coyote.

"Not yet. You have not done all that I require."

"What more must I do?" Coyote whined.

"The man who marries me must die four times and come to life again."

"Do you speak the truth? Do you mean that if I die four times and come to life four times you will marry me?"

"Yes," replied Beautiful Woman.

"Do you promise not to think up new tasks for me to do?" asked Coyote.

"That is all I ask."

Four times Coyote asked the same question and when she gave the same answer the fourth time he said, "Now you can kill me."

She led him outside her hogan and told him to lie down. Then she took a heavy club and hit him over the head. She beat him on the back and on the legs and all over his body until he was thoroughly crushed. Only the tip of his nose and the tip of his tail were untouched.

"Now Coyote is dead," she laughed, throwing down her club. And she returned to the hogan for she had much work to do. Later that day while she was weaving, she saw someone come to the doorway of her hogan. She looked up, and there she saw the figure of Coyote.

"I have won the first time," he said. "Three more times I die, and then I claim you for my wife."

Beautiful Woman did not say anything, but again she went outside the hogan and picked up a big club; she bade him lie down. Again she beat Coyote to a pulp. This time she picked up the pieces of his body, threw them in all directions, and went inside to resume her weaving. Then she saw him once more standing in the doorway, as if he had never been beaten to a pulp and thrown in all directions.

Coyote said, "Now I have won two games. If I win twice more, you will be my wife."

Beautiful Woman took no chances the third time— she beat Coyote until he was nothing but flayed fur, and the wind had blown him in the four earthly directions. However, luckily for Coyote, she had neglected to crush the tip of his tail and the tip of his nose. It was some time before Coyote could get himself together again, but he was by no means dead, and by evening he came round a third time and grinned in Beautiful Woman's face.

Now Beautiful Woman was truly afraid, because no living thing could withstand her beatings, and Coyote always came back as good as new. The fourth time Beautiful Woman mashed Coyote with a cornmeal masher, ground him into meal, and satisfied that he was finally done for and she was free to marry someone less clever and more easily controlled, she went inside to finish her weaving.

It took Coyote the longest time of his life to pull

himself together this last time, but he succeeded as before, because his nose-tip and the tip of his tail were intact and unharmed.

When Beautiful Woman looked up to see the moon she thought she saw Coyote standing in it, his head and shoulders all silvery and smooth.

"Coyote, is that you?" she asked fearfully, not believing what she saw.

And Coyote stepped down from his high rock perch, wearing a mantle of moonlight on his fur, and he said two words;

"I win."

And it was the truth.

TWO

INTRODUCTION TO PART TWO

A Navajo man, while herding his sheep, was overcome by an acute headache, returned to his hogan, and went to bed; a diviner was summoned to determine the cause of the pain and what had to be done for a cure. The diviner, an experienced hand trembler, determined that the cause of the headache was a snake, accidentally killed many years before. A chant, called an Evilway Chant, conducted by a specific singer, was given, and many relatives and friends came. At the end of the five days, the man was cured and harmony was restored.

Navajo ceremonies are centered around the maintenance of harmony (as in the Blessingway, used at the birth of a new baby, the change from girlhood to womanhood, or the blessing of a new hogan), or they are used, most commonly, to cure a person of a physical illness, a disturbed mental state, or bewitchment. Harmony and balance are essential to the Navajo world; when a person has disrupted this harmony, even if unknowingly, he will become ill. He can be cured only through the proper ceremony (referred to as a chant, a sing, or a way), which, as it recites some portion of the Origin Myth and symbolically recreates the world, also recreates the patient, harmoniously free of his past errors.

For the Navajos, sickness has two sides. There is that which is obvious: the extremely bad headache, the broken leg, the deep depression. And there is that which caused the obvious illness: the broken taboo, the offended Holy People, the disruption of harmony — waiting for the weakened physical state to let itself be known.

There are more than fifty chants or ways among the Navajo ceremonials. Each has its specific purpose, and most are highly complex, containing many different songs and rituals, which must be carried out perfectly. A ceremony held incorrectly by a singer (or medicine man) can bring evil or death to the patient. The chants are so complicated that most singers will learn only one in a lifetime.

Some of the ones often used today are the Beautyway, the Windways, and the Holyways.

In each Way, some portion of the Origin Myth will be retold. The basic plot is that of an individual, usually a youth, who leaves his home, often in search of adventure. During this search, he will go against the sanctions of the Holy People, either knowingly or out of ignorance, and for this he is punished. To redeem himself, he must fulfill the demands of the Holy People and undergo certain trials. Once these demands have been fulfilled, the youth is taught songs by the Holy People which give him supernatural power. He is instructed to return to his home, where he is warmly welcomed as the prodigal son, teaches the new songs to his people, and then chooses to return to live with the Holy People.

Two skilled members of the tribe are usually needed in the cure of a sick person. One is the diviner and the other is the singer, or medicine man. It is the diviner who determines the cause of the illness, what chant should be used as a cure, and which singer is the most suited to carry out the ceremony. In Navajo there is no general word for diviner, but there is a word which means "that which he knows." Divining, common to most cultures, is the innate ability to gain knowledge beyond the five senses, and the people who have this ability are regarded as holy and powerful.

Navajo diviners are divided into three categories: hand-tremblers, star (or sun) gazers, and listeners.* Few

---

*Listening as a means of diagnosing is only rarely used among the Navajos today. Like star-gazing, no innate psychic powers are used: it must be learned. The ritual is conducted without the aid of sand paintings or fetishes; instead, the listener dips his finger into a powder made from the dried ear drum of a badger and puts a bit of this powder into his own ears. Taking another man with him, he goes outside the hogan and prays to "listening." He sings and then waits to "hear" the cause of the illness. Many sounds are significant: the rattle of a rattlesnake, the roar of a bear, the crash of thunder. The sound of a person crying means that the patient will die.

Navajos remain today who are listeners, but hand-trembling and star-gazing are still widely used. Someone having these skills, usually a man, may also be a singer, but he is not necessarily one. Diviners can be used to find lost articles or to identify witches, but their talent is most commonly centered around sickness and its cause. If a person is "wise enough," the Navajos say, he will call for a diviner at the onset of his illness; still, it is their practice to wait until a series of medicine men have tried and failed. Because of the duality of illness, two medicine men may be prescribed by the diviner—one for the obvious manifestation of the illness and one for the underlying cause, the disharmony or broken rule.

When a hand-trembler is called in, he will ask a small fee, generally no more than a few dollars. He washes his hands and forearms and with one arm bared to the elbow, sits cross-legged near the patient. Sometimes he will sprinkle corn pollen on the patient and on his bare arm. Except for the pollen, no other accessories, such as fetishes, are used.

Next, he says a prayer to the Gila Monster's spirit, asking for information about the sickness and its cure. The Gila Monster is thought to know everything and to see everything. It is he who taught hand-trembling to The People. They know this because his forefoot shakes when he lifts it in walking.

The prayer is followed by several minutes of singing. During the prayer, the diviner sits with eyes closed; then, at the beginning of the singing, his hand begins to shake. The diviner thinks of different diseases, chants, medicine men. Something ("that which he knows") tells him which ones are right. At this, the shaking stops, the ceremony is over, and he announces what he has learned.

The source of the disease can be located by the trembling hand traveling over the body of the patient and stopping involuntarily at the afflicted spot. The proper medicine man is identified by the trembling hand pointing at his home. The proper chant comes when the hand moves freely in the sand in front of the diviner and, like automatic writing, indicates the name of the chant.

Hand-tremblers have described the feeling which comes over their arm as similar to that of your hand falling asleep, a tingling sensation, or one similar to an electric shock. This skill cannot be inherited or learned, but comes suddenly, like a gift.

Star-gazing, unlike hand-trembling, can be learned from a practitioner of the art. The star-gazer will go outside the hogan of the patient and sing to a specific star. Soon, this star will throw out a string of light ("like a motion picture") which tells the cause of the illness. White or yellow light, or light directed on the hogan, indicates that the patient will recover; red light means serious illness; if the hogan is shown as dark or burning, then death is imminent. The light of the star will point to the direction of the proper medicine man.

It is the singer or medicine man who conducts the chant and does the actual healing. He is highly trained, from having apprenticed himself to another singer for many years, before practicing on his own. After his training, he must undergo his particular ceremony, just as a psychoanalyst is required to undergo analysis before he can practice. He must know all the songs of the chant perfectly, each story, each step in the ritual—for there is so much power in his knowledge, that if he makes a mistake, he may lose the patient's life.

Because of the power which he holds, the medicine man is highly esteemed and regarded with a certain amount of fear. He often possesses a charismatic personality. He learns basic healing arts, hypnosis, massage, and many "magic" tricks, such as being able to pull a bone out of a patient's ear. Most important, however, is his ability to instill confidence in his patient, to make the patient feel that he is being cured. When a medicine man loses this ability, his career is over.

During the healing ceremony, the relationship between the medicine man and the patient is very close. The patient is sung over, touched, painted, sprinkled with pollen, massaged. They are together throughout the ceremony, whether it is a brief, one-day sing, or a full, nine-day sing. The patient is also surrounded by his family and friends, who witness and share in his rebirth. This feeling of intimacy and sharing, which the ceremony creates, is very important, for it helps to place the patient back within the harmony of his family and community, as well as within his universe.

Once an old Navajo was asked why he still preferred going to medicine men, rather than to the modern white doctors at the nearest hospital. His reply was that, in the hospital, the doctor hardly ever saw you, he barely touched you or talked to you. None of your family was present, and all you did was lie alone. In a Navajo ceremony, family, friends, and medicine man stay together throughout the ceremony, and the medicine man treats the entire body rather than just one part of it.

The sand painting, one of the most important aspects of a healing ceremony, is a dry painting made by the singer and his helpers on the clean swept floor of the hogan. It is through this intricate and colorful design, made from colors which are sacred to the Navajo—black, red, yellow, white, and turquoise—that the Holy People are approached. The designs made in the sand painting are traditional representations of the portion of the Origin Myth which is being recited. There is a border around the painting with an opening, which, like the single thread leading out from the center of a Navajo blanket, is a symbolic exit, so that the Holy People cannot be trapped by the humans, nor the humans trapped with them.

During the course of the ceremony, the patient sits

upon the sand painting while he is sung over. It is here, at this moment, that the patient is symbolically reborn with the universe, with Dineh, and as an individual. After the ceremony, the sand painting is destroyed, and the patient is restored to his normal state.

In the Navajo world, the present is the most meaningful, for in a circle there is no beginning and no end, and the most important point is where you stand at the moment. Navajos do not concern themselves with a life after death, nor do they spend the present preparing themselves for an afterlife. If they concern themselves with rules and rituals, it is because they do not want the harmony of the moment to be disturbed. Therefore, a man's death is not an overriding fear for him.

The dead, and contact with a dead body, are an entirely different matter. The Navajos believe that when a person dies, the good part of him travels away, but the evil part remains as a ghost to harass the living—especially those who may have given offense during the person's lifetime. Hogans in which someone has died are deserted or burned. Oddly enough, one of the greatest services given by the modern hospitals built on the Navajo reservation is that the dying can be taken there, and once death has occurred, the Navajo family can leave the body for disposal by the hospital staff.

ALICE WINSTON

Two
Medicine
Stories

Gila Monster's Tobacco

Gila Monster lived in a cave in a small, white rock canyon, where he grew two different kinds of wild tobacco. He would sit by the hour in the doorway of his cave watching the strong young plants and smoking a big pipe. He was one of the largest of the lizard family, everyone thought him very ugly, and that is why he was called Monster. From a lizard's point of view, however, he was quite handsome, with his jagged red and black markings and his scaly hide.

As I say, he enjoyed nothing under the sun so much as smoking, but he was not very generous with his tobacco. He thought it was too fine to waste on common folk, and he gave it as presents to only one or two of his friends. One was Bull Frog who lived in the green pool beside the cave. He did not care for smoking as much as Gila Monster. But he liked a puff now and then. He would pop up to the surface of the green pool and say in a deep, throaty voice, "Cousin Gila Monster, give me a puff of your fine tobacco."

Whereupon Gila Monster would reply, "Certainly, Cousin Bull Frog. Have your choice."

It was amusing to watch the big frog smoke. He sat on his favorite stone and held his pipe awkwardly in his wide frog mouth. The remarkable part was that every time he took a puff, the smoke poured out through the brown spots on his back. It looked for all the world as if he were on fire. Gila Monster never tired of watching the smoke come out of his friend's back. He enjoyed it almost as much as smoking himself. After Bull Frog had puffed for a while he would return the big pipe and say, "Thank you, Cousin," and with a splash he would jump back into his green pool.

Another person who was privileged to have a bit of Gila Monster's famous tobacco was Chipmunk. He lived in a crack of rock above Gila Monster's cave and he had an agreement with him which said that if he carried the fresh-picked tobacco leaves and spread them to dry in the sun, Gila Monster would let the little fellow keep a bundle for himself. Chipmunk smoked corn silk tassels if he ran out of tobacco.

One time the ground squirrels, mountain squirrels, red squirrels, and grey squirrels all visited Chipmunk on the same day. He rolled cigarettes of the choice tobacco for his guests.

"Where did you get this fine-smelling smoke?" they asked.

"From my neighbor, Gila Monster," replied Chipmunk with pride. "He gives me a small sack for drying his leaves."

Soon the guests had smoked every flake. Chipmunk did not know what to do. He wanted to please his friends, but he did not have another tobacco smoke for them.

"Stay here," he said to the squirrels, "and smoke corn silk tassels. I'm going to slip down to Gila Monster's fields and get tobacco for you."

When Chipmunk returned with plenty of tobacco the squirrels sat and smoked for hours until immense blue clouds poured out of the windows; for three whole days the squirrels smoked without stopping.

In the meantime, Gila Monster began to wonder what his little friend was doing. For three days he had not come to spread leaves to dry and for three days Gila Monster had not caught a glimpse of Chipmunk's tail. On the fourth day he went to walk in his fields and there he saw that many leaves had been stripped from his precious plants.

"Who has been stealing my tobacco?" he shouted. "Fly, come, I have a job for you!"

Now, it was Fly who guarded the fields for Gila Monster, and he was buzzing around in the far end of the canyon. He knew that Chipmunk had been stealing tobacco, but since Chipmunk always gave plenty to him, he promised not to tell—when Gila Monster called to him, however, he was very frightened. He buzzed close to Gila Monster's ears:

"Look at the smoke coming out of Chipmunk's windows," he whispered.

Gila Monster sniffed the wind which bore from that direction. "Smells like my tobacco smoke," he said.

"Look at the tracks in the earth," said Fly. "I can tell you who the thief is: it's Chipmunk. He did it while you were asleep." And away buzzed Fly.

Gila Monster examined the tracks. "That is surely Chipmunk's foot," he said to himself. Then he called loudly for Chipmunk to come down to his cave. "Time to dry more leaves," he shouted in a gruff voice.

Chipmunk left his guests to their smoking and hurried to the home of the big lizard.

"Is that your footprint?" Gila Monster asked, pointing to the track in the earth. Chipmunk was scared to death.

"I'm not the only one with a foot like that," he piped.

"Tell me the truth," hissed Gila Monster.

"I didn't steal your tobacco," lied the little fellow.

"All right. Go home, then," said Gila Monster, satisfied.

Chipmunk went home very much relieved. He decided that he would never steal again as long as he lived. But the next day who should drop in to visit him but Mountain Squirrel. He had with him two bags of delicious piñon nuts to trade for tobacco.

"I'll steal just once more," he said under his breath. "But never again after today."

Then he ran down the rocks to the fields of Gila Monster and came back with two sacks of fine tobacco leaves to trade for piñon nuts. Mountain Squirrel was pleased with the bargain, and so was Chipmunk, but no sooner had he finished his deal, than he heard the voice of Gila Monster calling.

"Come here, Chipmunk. I want to talk to you."

Chipmunk was frozen in his tracks. He didn't want to face the big lizard, but he dared not refuse.

When he got to the cave, Gila Monster said, "I know that you are the thief. Fly saw you. It is no use for you to lie."

"I didn't steal your tobacco, Gila Monster, I swear I didn't!"

Now Gila Monster was a witch, who knew how to cast spells over people, and he cast a spell over Chipmunk right then and there. "If you lie," he said, "your feet will dry up."

"I didn't steal," repeated Chipmunk in a daze.

That night he felt very sick. His feet itched and shrunk and shriveled; he lit a cigarette but the smoke made him dizzy. At midnight he was so sick that he sent for Star Gazer, who went into a trance. Star Gazer knew how to tell what diseases people have, and he soon found out what was wrong with Chipmunk.

"You are bewitched," he said simply. "The only person that can cure you is the witch who cast a spell over you."

Chipmunk felt his shriveled feet and he remembered the words of Gila Monster.

"The witch is old Gila Monster," said Chipmunk.

"We must go to him," said Star Gazer. "We will take him a present."

"There is deer meat in the store room," said Chipmunk, too sick to move.

Star Gazer made a bundle of deer meat and wrapped little Chipmunk in a blanket. Then he carried the deer meat and the sick little fellow to the cave of Gila Monster, who sat in his doorway, smoking his great pipe and paying no attention to the present which was laid at his feet. He kept on smoking his pipe; at last he motioned his guests to go inside. Star Gazer laid Chipmunk on the floor, still wrapped in the blanket.

"I will never steal again," said Chipmunk in a shrunken, quavering voice.

Gila Monster looked at him. "All right, little one," he said, "see that you don't. Now I will cure you." He took an herb from his witch's medicine bundle and put a pinch of it in the monster pipe. He handed the pipe to Chipmunk, who was so tiny that all but his ears were hidden behind the huge bowl. He gave one weak puff, which made his head spin like a pebble in the river.

"Take another puff," commanded Gila Monster.

The second time the smoke tasted better; the third time he no longer felt dizzy; the fourth time he felt cured and jumped out of the blanket and whisked about the cave doing a little dance. Then he looked down at his feet.

"Look!" he cried in distress, "My feet are still shriveled!"

"That is to remind you not to steal or lie," said Gila Monster, and from that day on Chipmunk dried Gila

Monster's tobacco leaves. After work, he smoked one pipeful, which he had earned, but he never would steal or lie, or take more than his share.

And to this day all Chipmunks have tiny feet.

Humming Bird, the Medicine Man

A long time ago the birds came together in council to appoint a medicine man. They sat in a circle around Big Pine. The warblers, the mocking birds, the yellow birds, the blackbirds, the bluebirds, and the humming bird.

"We need someone to take care of us when we get sick," said Blackbird. Now as everyone knows, Humming Bird knows all of the beautiful flowers, the herbs, and the grasses. He spends his life dipping into blossoms and sucking out honey with his pointed bill. Hosteen Yazzi, the other birds call him, which in Navajo means Little Fellow. True enough, he is very small but he is also wise.

After much chattering, all of the birds agreed that Humming Bird was the most learned, even if he was the smallest, and they appointed him to be Medicine Man.

Humming Bird dashed about on his delicate wings with enormous pride; he sucked out the juices of many plants to make medicine. Then he flew to the mountains, and there he gathered the cups of acorn nuts, which he stored with the medicines in a hole in Big Pine, his home.

Soon, Blackbird, Yellow Bird, Mocking Bird, and Warbler came to visit him. Between them was Bluebird, who was too sick to fly. He was sitting in his nest, which the other birds carried between them.

"Here is your first patient," they said. "Bluebird is sick."

Humming Bird fluttered over the nest. "Call our friends together. At dawn we shall have a sing," he said.

The four birds flew up into the sky, and when the dawn light came, birds of all kinds flew down to Big Pine. Blackbirds, Yellow Birds, Warblers, and Mocking Birds made a circle around Bluebird.

At the break of day they began to chant and pray; each sang his own song, except for Mocking Bird who sang a little of everyone else's song, since he did not have one of his own. What warbling and singing!

Humming Bird sat in the middle of the circle beside the nest, looking no larger than a moth. Before him, he set 32 acorn cups filled with medicines. In his hand, he held the red flower which is like sacred corn pollen to the birds. He shook it gently over Bluebird and every once in a while he gave the patient a drink from an acorn cup.

For four days the birds came at dawn, settled in a great circle around sick Bluebird, and sang. For four days Humming Bird shook the red flower over his head and gave his patient medicines. At dawn of the fourth day Bluebird hopped out of his nest and was well again.

"I am cured," he sang. At sunrise he flew into the blue sky singing the song of the bluebirds.

The others flapped their wings in excitement. "Humming Bird is a fine medicine man," they said, and ever since that day they have called on Humming Bird to cure their diseases. At the break of day you can always hear birds singing for one of their sick friends.

Old Navajo medicine men tell how their fathers used the song of Humming Bird for a prayer over their own sick ones. But now the old prayers are forgotten, and only Humming Bird remembers the words to his song.

Chants, Dances, Dawns, and Prayers: Sixteen Poems of Navajo Ceremony

Sitting on the Blue-Eyed Bear

Inside the hogan
colored earths make bear tracks
leading in,
bear tracks and sunlight—
sun dogs
at the four quarters.
Bear is soaked in sunlight
in the center.
Twigs at the entrance of Bear's den
are trees.

The sick person has a vision of Bear
when he sits upon painted sand.
Then Bear-man
rushes into the hogan, snarling and growling.
All the sitting people join in—
this is the moment
when the women faint.

The White Man's Ghost

White man's ghost which threatens
    my clouds.
White man's ghost which knows
    no resting place.
White man's ghost which comes
    and goes on skittery feet,
pawing at my body places:
    my suns, my spruces, my clouds.

I will wear now those dark flints
that protect,
I will dance as they rattle
upon my skin.

The dark bear: I borrow the flints
of his furred hands,
the soaring eagle: I borrow the flints
of her feathered hands.

Now I will wash my body's house
in the pollen that rests on blue ponds.
A fine yellow pollen, water pollen
makes my skin shine,
makes my heart great
so that the white man's ghost
will no longer threaten
my suns, my spruces, my clouds.

The Making of
Cornfather-Dancer's Headdress

Go find the hide of a deer
not killed by a weapon.

Draw the cutting-lines for the skin
with a piece of crystal.

Use the sinew from the right side
of the spinal column
for sewing the right side of the headdress.

Yellow feathers from the little yellow bird
are sewn on the right side
and the whole work
is done by a righthanded man.

Now for the left,
use the sinew from that side
of the spinal column.
A lefthanded man will sew bluebird feathers
on the left side of the headdress.

The right-side-feathers
are for the Black Water Jar
which brings rain.
The left-side-feathers
are for the ears of corn.

The dancer with the headdress
is called Corn Father.

Flute Boy Watches
a Hopi Butterfly Dance

The young men,
the young women
stand in a circle.

The young women
wear white robes
tied at one shoulder
with one arm bare.

They wear headdresses
made of black-painted boards.
Butterflies and white flowers
float on the headdresses.

Now the butterflies come
on tireless wings;
rested and bright
their wings open in desert air.

The voices sing:

"We are young, the corn is green
we chase the yellow sun
we play with golden butterfly girls."

Between

Between the first frost of autumn
and the third moon of winter

something lives between:
it has eyes that hear,
ears that see

with beads and waters and pollens
it breathes, sings, dances—

it lives
between
like a knife
stuck in a rock

None may go unclean
between
the haunted breath of autumn
the second wind of winter.

Winter Thunder

Winter thunder
makes my separate parts
scatter

First, my breath is gone, caged and rasping
by old willows,
then my bones and teeth
are blown to the twelve winds!
My ribs gone, my pelvis, my spine,
my collarbone, my tailbone—
sadly do I lose my bones!

My saliva and hair is gone, buried
in dry lizard rocks!
My skin, blasted, ripped
by forks of lightning!

My vitals, my spleen, my liver—
all but my heart—blown and spiked
on cactus thorns.
I see them there, but cannot touch them.
I must call them back,
I must beckon their return
with gifts of pollen.

In several whirlwinds they come back:
when I stand in the center of my broad cornfield
beautified with white corn, yellow corn
with corn pollen, with grasshoppers
and the hundred corn-carrying beetles.

My parts return to me through the tips of my fingers.
They return to their place of birth,
they enter the round cave that is me.
My bones and teeth and saliva
and hair and skin . . .
all return, all forgiven, all given back.

And I ask of them: did you like the Places of the Night
where Winter Thunder took you and shook you,
before you came home?

And my bones refuse to answer.

The Man

Man who walks when the dog will
not bite him.
Man who cups the stars in his palms.
Man whose bare feet are tickled
by snakes' tongues . . .

"This Man, I call him,
I have need of him.
Bring him to me, for I am sick
and will die unless he comes
and tells me what is ailing.
His medicine is strong,
he will tell me if I live or die."

The lamb was given in exchange
and The Man Who Looks Into The Sun
came to look at a young girl.
He stared directly
into the heart of a star
and sang.
He kept looking at that star.
Then it broke open
before his eyes
and he saw a blazing hogan
come out of it.

"That means the girl will die."

And in less than one month
she was dead.

Man who walks with stars drawn
upon his skin.
Man whose hands are early blessed
by pollen.
Man who sees no one trapped
in the sun.

"Man, O, Man
I have need of you,
for I am another
about to die.
Come, sing me well,
come sing me!"

The lamb was given
and another's daughter was visited
by the Man.
He sat quiet by folds
of moonwhite sheep fur
and stared into the girl's eyes.
"Tonight, a white sign comes around
the hogan like frost,
that means she will be well
within a week."

And she was.

"Man who is brother of white winds
and black fogs,
I have strewn sands in your hogan
and eaten pollen-balls made by your hands;

but my hands do not move
when I gaze and sing:
does that mean I may never see signs?"

The Man answered "Yes."

Coarse Hair's Medicine

1

Coarse Hair sat at the right
of the altar
and sang seven songs
to scatter ghosts
of the Ancient People
whose bones were lying around.

2

In a horn in his medicine pouch
was deer fat, fat of the mountain sheep,
fat of the mountain lion, wolf, otter:
all these Coarse Hair rolled into a ball
and laid down upon a stone.

3

A single crow's feather,
a feather of the turkey buzzard
were laid down
next to the ball of fat.

4

With yucca leaves, Coarse Hair
kneaded the body of Tall Man
at finger ends, shoulder and head,
and at the fifteen body places.
Then came the dead crow head-scratcher,
the roadrunner's tailfeather
sprinkled with pollen,
black grease on the fifteen body places,
ashes on the bones of the ancients,
feathers on the jaw,
the blackening of the face.

5

Then Coarse Hair placed dirt
'from a gopher's hole
into Tall Man's mocassins
and his wife's—
she placed hers on the outside of the hogan.

6

Coarse Hair killed the ghost
by pointing four times
toward the ashes on the bones
with a crowsbill.
Then he pointed the crowsbill
at the sky four times
and inhaled from the sun
with hands cupping his mouth.

7

This was how Coarse Hair's medicine
killed the ghost of a Ute
whose body was killed in battle
by Tall Man.

Medicines and Injuries

*If an old man counts the petals
of his age
he will die.*

*If a man whistles at night
the dead will draw near
and do harm.*

*If a man dreams his horse dies,
he will get sick.*

*If a man dreams teeth are pulled,
he will die.*

If a man swallows
a woman's monthly blood,
he will break a bone.

If a man makes a mistake
in learning Night Chant
he will be paralyzed.

But if a man avoids these things,
if he does not put strain
in his life,
if he follows his father's path
in wisdom,
he will live long and well,
pollen will shine in his smile
and stars will dance
like moths over his hogan.

The Risen Sun:
Woman's Ceremony

Changing Woman
was born of Horizontal Woman
and Upper Darkness.
Found on a mountain top, she was
taken home by a stranger.
In twelve days,
she was a big girl.
In eighteen days,
a complete woman.

"I am called Peach Blossom.
On this night,
all in the hogan stay awake
until the dawn
when the singers of songs
sing the Dawn Songs
of Changing Woman.
Now the curtain of the hogan
is torn aside and I run out
toward the south for half a mile.
Six young men follow me and
pretend to race; I know I will
beat them and this will bring
much good luck.

When I return, the ashes are
blown off the corncake
and a woman cuts a circle out of the center
and divides this into parts.
I take one and present it to
Boy-Who-Looks-Down.

He avoids my eyes,
but he accepts the
corncake and takes a small
nibble of it. Now the sun
is risen. I am a Woman.''

Washing Hands and Hair: The Wedding

It happens that a man sends two relatives
to the girl's hogan.

When they see soot around the smokehole,
or when it is wet around the fireplace
they ask if their relative may marry there.

Ponies are presented to the girl's parents.

On the wedding day,
the bride dips water
from a pot with a gourd ladle
and pours it over the groom's hands.
Then he pours water over
the bride's hands.

A wedding basket is passed to the groom
who eats a fingerful of mush
from the east side of the basket,
the south, the west, the north,
and the center;
the bride does the same.

The feast lasts until dawn.
Then the newly married couple have a race—
the one who wins will be rich.

In two or three days,
they wash each other's hair with yucca suds
and then, they begin their life as one.

Birth

The mother sits on a sheepskin
in the hogan.
Close at hand are her mother
and her sister: one holds her hips,
another her knees.
A medicine man touches her
with a feather while he sings.

After the moment of birth—
after the cord is tied—
the newborn is taken outside
and bathed with yucca suds
in a pile of ashes.

When the child is frail, it is rubbed
with sage and sung over—
and if it cries, all is well.

When the child won't cry,
it is placed in a piñon tree
and no one ever goes near it again.

The Chanter's Failure

When the Night Chant fails nine times,
I step into a piñon fire
made by my own hands
in a moth's trance,
and splash my bones
with fiery blue water—
only when the flames
have blackened me clean,
will the ash of guilt
blow far, far away
from my grandfather's
father's home.

Houses of the Gods

The house of the Gods
is a house made of dawns
or a house made of moss
or a house made of cottons
or a house made of rain
or a house made of suns·
or a house made of turquoise
or a house made of winds
or a house made of fur
or a house made of pollens
or a house made of flint
or a house made of crystals

Gods of all houses under heavens,
Bless my house made of mud, resin, and pine.
Bless my family made of blood, marrow, and b

Prayer Before the Night Chant of "All is Well"

For long years I have kept
this beauty within me.
It has been my life.
Now it is given
as the gift of dew is given by the sky
or the pollen from the cornflower.
My days have been long.
May the days of those who listen
be made longer.
I give so that no harm comes.
I make offerings
of pollen
of dew.

Song from
the Chant "All is Well"

All is beautiful before me
behind me
below me
above me
all is beautiful all around me.

This covers all,
the mountains
whose ways are beautiful,
the skies
the waters
the darkness
the dawn
whose ways are beautiful,
whose ways are beautiful
all around me.

ABOUT THE POEMS

Sitting on the Blue-Eyed Bear

This poem refers to the Mountain Top Way, which is directly translated to mean "a chant towards a place within the mountains." Since bears live in the mountains, they are the major power in the Mountain Top Way. The Navajos have a strong fear of the power of the bear. In spite of mythological references to his being good (he and Snake Man were guardians of Sun's house, protectors of Changing Woman, and were given by Changing Woman to The People to guard them on their journeys) he must also be reckoned with as potentially dangerous. After having done much good for the people, he began to cause coughs and bad luck and aligned himself with evil. Because of this he and his relatives were assigned to walk in Black Mountain where there have since been many bears.

Many chants have an accessory rite know as the shock rite. It is referred to in this poem when Bear Man enters and the women faint. The purpose of this shock rite is to induce and correct symptoms due to the contemplation of supernatural things too strong for the patient. Bear Man represents dangers and sufferings encountered by the Holy Man. His effect is intended to eliminate fear and inspire confidence.

The purpose of the Mountain Top Way is to remove all bad effects caused by bears. It is to cure disease, invoke unseen powers on behalf of The People for rain and good crops and to perpetuate the religious symbolism. By sitting on the sand painting described in the poem, the sick person draws strength and is healed.

The Mountain Top Way can be celebrated only in the winter when thunder is silent and the rattlesnake is hibernating. To relate the tales at any other time would bring death from lightning or a snake bite.

The White Man's Ghost

The ghosts of the dead can cause harm to the living, especially if the living had offended the dead sometime before their death. The ghost wanders at night and can cause physical illness, misfortune, or mental anguish as forms of revenge. The Enemy Way is needed to rid the victim of the power of the ghost.

The fear of the white man, perhaps murdered by the speaker, is threatening him, and ritual steps must be taken to exorcise the evil spirit. On yet another level, the white man's ghost refers to an alien culture which has threatened and continues to threaten the Navajos.

The Making of Cornfather-Dancer's Headdress

Right and Left may refer back to the Twin Slayers, sons of Changing Woman. The bold, right side (representing the Sun Father) is the masculine twin, the one who takes the initiative in legendary encounters. The left side (representing Earth, Mother, Moon) is the weaker of the two and more shy; he walks to the left, on the heart side. This sense of dichotomy is expressed in Frank Waters' *Masked Gods*.

Flute Boy Watches a Hopi Butterfly Dance

The Hopi, whose dance Flute Boy is watching, are one of the oldest of the Pueblo Indians. Their villages, one of which is over one thousand years old, are situated on Black Mesa in the center of Navajo country. Because of their proximity, they have had a great influence on the Navajo. They are known as the people of peace. Black Mesa, which is sacred to the Hopi and the Navajo (figuring in both their mythologies), is being strip-mined today and has a large power plant operating on it.

Between

The Winter Ceremonies, which last about four months, cannot be celebrated in summer when snakes, bears, and lightning are prevalent. They begin when the ground freezes in October.

Winter Thunder

This poem suggests the long and involved Flint Way, where the hero seduces the wife of White Thunder, who later shatters him with a bolt of lightning. According to the myth, Gila Monster is the singer who restores the hero by cutting his own body into tiny pieces and throwing them in all directions; Gila Monster is restored by the Wind People, Sunlight People, and other Holy People.

Thus the singer heals himself, and is therefore enabled to heal someone else: in the myth, he restores the shattered hero.

The Man

This poem refers to the diviners, the gifted of the tribe, who have a perception beyond the normal. They include Hand Tremblers, Star Gazers, and Listeners. Because hand-trembling is an innate ability and cannot be taught or learned, the speaker in the final stanza cannot become a practitioner. No matter how many rituals he may fulfill, the power must come from inside him.

The Risen Sun: Woman's Ceremony

Changing Woman is the most popular of the Holy People. She is the only one who constantly works positively for

The People and has never done them harm. She represents all the ideal qualities of woman: birth, death, and regeneration. The poem concerns the rite of passage, which still occurs in Navajo society and is often depicted in paintings. This is the puberty ceremony, which is given Navajo girls when they reach womanhood. It was given for Changing Woman at the time of her first menstrual cycle. When Navajo girls undergo this ceremony, they become, like Changing Woman, symbols of beauty and regeneration.

Birth

In many cultures, each change of life is marked with a ceremony. So with the Navajo. At birth, the child is welcomed or initiated into the Navajo world.

The dead child is placed in a tree and not looked upon because of the fear of death. If the child is born dead and utters no cry, then the four days of ceremonial mourning are not necessary, since the ghost had no opportunity to be offended or to become angry.

The Chanter's Failure

Chanters (singers or medicine men, the terms are interchangeable) are powerful men of the tribe because they hold the knowledge of sacred rituals and thus commune with the Holy People. Since they can use this power to help a person, they can also use it to harm someone. Much of the chanter's success lies in his ability to instill confidence in his patient. If his chants fail and the patient is not cured, then his power is gone, and he is no longer called upon to conduct chants.

A.W.

Bibliography

Adair, John. *The Navajo and Pueblo Silversmiths.*
University of Oklahoma Press, 1944.

Adams, William Y. "Navajo Social Organization."
American Anthropologist, 73:1 (1970),
pp. 273-277.

Curtis, Edward S. *The North American Indian.*
Johnson Reprint Corporation, 1970.

Dyk, Walter. *Son of Old Man Hat.*
University of Nebraska Press, 1938.

Eliade, Mircea. *Myth and Reality.*
Harper and Row, 1963.

Hassell, Grace. *Bessie Yellowhair.*
Warner Books, 1974.

Hillerman, Tony. *The Blessing Way.*
Harper and Row, 1972.

Hogner, Dorothy Childs. *Navajo Winter Nights.*
Thomas Nelson and Sons, 1935.

Metcalf, Paul. *Will West.*
The Bookstore Press, 1973.

Momaday N. Scott. *House Made of Dawn.*
New American Library, 1969.

Moon, Sheila. *A Magic Dwells.*
Wesleyan University Press, 1970.

Newcomb, Franc Johnson. *Navajo Neighbors.*
University of Oklahoma Press, 1966.

O'Bryan, Aileen. *The Dine: Origin Myths of the
Navajo Indians.* Smithsonian Institution,
Bureau of Ethnology Bulletin 163.

Pousma, Richard H. *He-Who-Always-Wins.*
William B. Eerdmans Publishing Co., 1934.

Reichard, Gladys A. *Prayer: The Compulsive Word.*
University of Washington Press, 1966.

Reichard, Gladys A. *Social Life of the Navajo Indians,*
Vol. III. Columbia University Press, 1928.

Snyder, Gary. *Myths and Texts.*
Corinth Books, 1959.

Spencer, Katherine. *Mythology and Values:*
An Analysis of Navajo Chantway Myths.
American Folklore Society, 1957.

Underhill, Ruth. *The Navajos.*
University of Oklahoma Press, 1956.

Waters, Frank. *Masked Gods,*
Navajo and Pueblo Ceremonialism.
Ballantine Books, 1970.

Wood, Nancy. *Hollering Sun.*
Simon and Schuster, 1972.

Wyman, Leland C. "New Diagnosticians,"
American Anthropologist, Vol. 38 (1936),
pp. 236-246.

Wyman, Leland C. *The Windways of the Navajo.*
The Taylor Museum of the Colorado
Springs Fine Arts Center, 1962.